FEDERAL FORCES
CAREERS AS
FEDERAL AGENTS

A CAREER AS A
SECRET SERVICE
AGENT

Therese Shea

PowerKiDS press.

New York

Published in 2016 by The Rosen Publishing Group, Inc.
29 East 21st Street, New York, NY 10010

First Edition

Editor: Caitlin McAneney
Book Design: Mickey Harmon

Photo Credits: Cover (image), p. 13 1000 images/Shutterstock.com; cover (logo) Color Symphony/Shutterstock.com; cover, pp. 1, 3–32 (mesh texture) Eky Studio/Shutterstock.com; p. 5 David Stuart Productions/Shutterstock.com; p. 7 ASSOCIATED PRESS/APImages.com; p. 9 Henry Griffin/Associated Pressr/APImages.com; p. 11 AFP/Stringer/Getty Images; p. 15 Chip Somodevilla / Staff/Getty Images; p. 16 Bloomberg / Contributor/Getty Images; p. 17 Mark J. Terrill/APImages.com; p. 19 mikeledray/Shutterstock.com; p. 20 Dmcdevit/Wikimedia Commons; p. 21 Photo 12 / Contributor/Getty Images; p. 22 Kevin Horan / Contributor/Getty Images; p. 23 The White House / Handout/Getty Images; p. 25 American Spirit/Shutterstock.com; p. 27 Dirck Halstead / Contributor/Getty Images; p. 29 PAUL J. RICHARDS/AFP/Getty Images; p. 30 Rommel Canlas/Shutterstock.com.

Library of Congress Cataloging-in-Publication Data

Shea, Therese.
 A career as a Secret Service agent / Therese Shea.
     pages cm. — (Federal forces : careers as federal agents)
Includes bibliographical references and index.
ISBN 978-1-4994-1062-4 (pbk.)
ISBN 978-1-4994-1098-3 (6 pack)
ISBN 978-1-4994-1117-1 (library binding)
1. United States. Secret Service—Juvenile literature. 2. Secret service—United States—Juvenile literature. I. Title.
 HV8144.S43S54 2016
 363.28'302373—dc23
                                    2015005708

Manufactured in the United States of America

CPSIA Compliance Information: Batch #WS15PK: For Further Information contact Rosen Publishing, New York, New York at 1-800-237-9932

Contents

Always Watching, Always Ready

The president steps onto the stage, ready to give a speech. A crowd of thousands is cheering and clapping. The noise is thunderous. People hang out of nearby buildings and stand on rooftops, trying to get a glimpse of this historic moment. Men and women surround the president. Some are family members, others are White House staff, and still others work in Congress.

A few of these people aren't known to the world. They wear dark suits and sunglasses. They have earpieces that are barely noticeable. Every once in a while, one raises a wrist to their mouth and says something. They're wearing hidden **microphones**! These mysterious men and women are Secret Service agents. They're responsible for keeping the president and others safe at all times.

Secret Service agents are always on the lookout for trouble. Many don't wear uniforms, so they're not always easy to spot.

The First Secret Service

The Secret Service wasn't founded to protect the American president, but to fight the spread of counterfeit, or fake, money. After the American Civil War (1861–1865), there was a lot of counterfeit money in use. Some think one-third of all U.S. money at that time was counterfeit! So, the Department of the Treasury established its Secret Service Division on July 5, 1865. The first chief was William P. Wood.

The agency was so effective that soon it was tackling more federal crimes, especially those in which the criminals were trying to cheat the government. These included **investigations** into mail theft and **smuggling**. The Federal Bureau of Investigation (FBI), founded in 1908, later took over many of these matters, but the Secret Service still handles many financial crimes.

The job of cleaning up U.S. currency, or money, after the Civil War was a hard one. About 1,600 state banks printed their own notes. Each note had a different design, making it hard to tell the 4,000 kinds of counterfeits from the 7,000 varieties of real money! Today, the whole nation uses the same design for its currency, and it's thought that less than 0.01 percent of American currency is counterfeit.

Secret Service agents found these counterfeit quarters on May 31, 1940, in an apartment in New York City.

The Secret Service Today

The Secret Service is now a federal agency that has operated within the Department of Homeland Security since 2003. Today, the agency is best known for providing protection for the U.S. president.

The Secret Service began guarding presidents part-time in 1894, beginning with President Grover Cleveland. After President William F. McKinley was **assassinated** in 1901, they provided full-time protection to each president.

Mission Statement

According to the official Secret Service website, the mission of the U.S. Secret Service is: "to ensure the security of our President, our Vice President, their families, the White House, the Vice President's Residence, national and visiting world leaders, former Presidents, and events of national significance. The Secret Service also protects the integrity of our currency and investigates crimes against our national financial system committed by criminals around the world and in cyberspace."

Other people receive protection, too. The president's family, the vice president and family, and visiting heads of foreign countries are assigned Secret Service agents. Those running for president and vice president also receive protection within 120 days of the election if they're well-known enough that they might be in danger.

After the assassination of presidential hopeful Robert F. Kennedy in 1968, the Secret Service began providing protection to certain candidates.

Secret Service Protection

The president and others under long-term protection of the Secret Service, called protectees, usually have special agents assigned to them. These agents are on "protection detail." They promise to guard people even in situations of life or death. That means they'll get between their protectee and danger, putting themselves in harm's way. A few agents have been shot while on protection detail.

Though Secret Service agents on protection detail are the most visible, most Secret Service agents do behind-the-scenes work. They investigate any threats made against their protectees to discover if they're serious or not. This may mean working on a computer, making telephone calls, or traveling around the world to meet with people. They report their findings back to the agency.

Former presidents, such as Bill Clinton, are protected by the Secret Service for the rest of their life.

When a president or other protectee travels, a team of Secret Service agents arrives where they're going ahead of time. They check with local law enforcement to find out if there are possible threats in the area. They make sure the president stays in the safest place. They also plan the best travel routes as well as emergency routes to get the president to a secure location in case something happens.

There aren't enough Secret Service agents to keep watch over everything. So, they work with local agencies, such as police and firefighters, to create a network of protectors who are in contact and sharing information at all times. Because so many people are on lookout, possible danger can be spotted in time more easily.

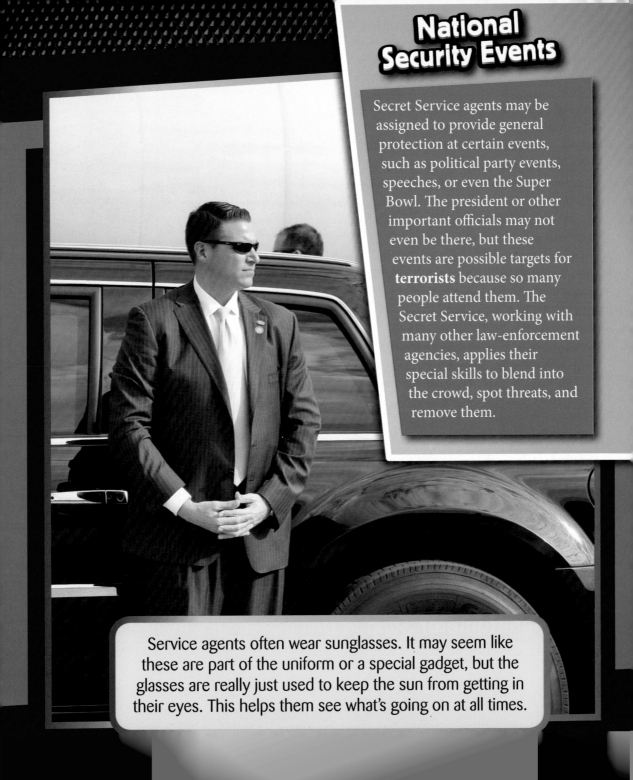

National Security Events

Secret Service agents may be assigned to provide general protection at certain events, such as political party events, speeches, or even the Super Bowl. The president or other important officials may not even be there, but these events are possible targets for **terrorists** because so many people attend them. The Secret Service, working with many other law-enforcement agencies, applies their special skills to blend into the crowd, spot threats, and remove them.

Service agents often wear sunglasses. It may seem like these are part of the uniform or a special gadget, but the glasses are really just used to keep the sun from getting in their eyes. This helps them see what's going on at all times.

The Secret Service also has a Uniformed Division that acts as a kind of police at the White House, the vice president's house, and other places in Washington, D.C. Uniformed Secret Service may be stationed at posts, such as the White House fence, or they may patrol areas on foot, by bicycle, or in vehicles.

The Uniformed Division includes the Countersniper Support Unit. These agents look for threats such as snipers, or hidden gunmen who shoot from a distance. The Canine Explosives Detection Unit uses dogs to sniff out bombs and other explosive devices. The Emergency Response Team is ready to spring into action in the event that a dangerous situation does occur. Away from the White House, the **Magnetometer** Support Unit makes sure no one near the protectee is armed.

Sometimes, the Countersniper Support Unit is seen with weapons on the White House roof.

Secret Service Investigation

Some Secret Service agents who aren't involved with protection focus their efforts on investigations involving U.S. currency. That may mean identifying counterfeit money. Counterfeit money can be even harder to spot now because of advanced computers and printers. However, many monetary dealings these days aren't even handled with paper money and coins. Instead, people use the Internet to pay for items, move money from bank to bank, and do other business that can take place at lightning speed.

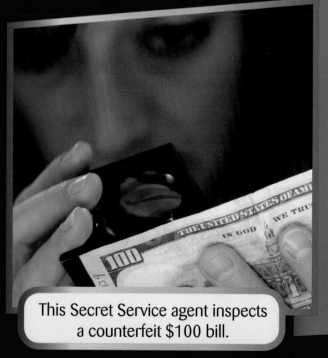

This Secret Service agent inspects a counterfeit $100 bill.

The Secret Service has had to learn how to be on the watch for financial crimes. Investigations may include finding people who are using false identities to take money from others. Other investigations may deal with examining computers for illegal programs that collect private information, such as bank account numbers.

Some computer files can be passed from computer to computer, where they "spy" on people for criminals. The Secret Service tracks down these criminals and their harmful computer files to stop them from stealing people's information.

In 2001, President George W. Bush ordered the Secret Service to establish the Electronic Crimes Task Forces. This nationwide network includes federal, state, and local law enforcement agencies as well as schools and private companies. All involved work together to prevent, detect, and investigate crimes involving the Internet, computers, or other electronic devices.

Besides using computers to investigate crimes, the Secret Service also has an amazing **forensic** lab. There they can identify fingerprints and use **polygraphs** to separate truths from lies. They have special tools to examine photographs, documents, and recorded voices, too.

The Secret Service's forensic lab is so advanced that agents may be called upon to help out other agencies such as the FBI. In fact, since 1994, the Secret Service has been providing forensic assistance to investigations involving missing children.

Secret Service: Two-Part Mission

protection duties	financial crime fighting
• president and family	• counterfeit currency detection
• vice president and family	• financial information theft
• visiting heads of foreign countries and spouses	• identity theft
• presidential and vice-presidential candidates	• government check theft
• certain national events	• financial crimes involving the Internet, computers, or other electronic devices
• former presidents	

Besides its agents, the Secret Service also uses the talents of scientists, computer specialists, photographers, writers, and lawyers.

Secret Service Heroics

Some Secret Service agents have made the greatest sacrifice in carrying out their duties—their own life. On November 1, 1950, two men walked up to the Blair House in Washington, D.C. President Harry Truman was staying there while work was being done on the White House. The men began shooting at the police and agents guarding the building.

One Secret Service agent, Leslie Coffelt, was shot three times. As he was losing **consciousness**, he managed to kill one of the attackers before the man could reach the president. The other man was shot, too, and the battle was over. Thirty shots had been fired in only three minutes. Coffelt died four hours later at the hospital. He's buried in Arlington National Cemetery in Virginia.

Harry S. Truman

Leslie Coffelt was just 40 years old when he gave his life to protect President Harry Truman.

On March 30, 1981, President Ronald Reagan was leaving a hotel in Washington, D.C. As he was walking to his car, his Secret Service detail began to group around him for protection. Suddenly, a man named John Hinckley Jr. came forward and fired. A bullet hit the president. Before Hinckley could shoot again, Agent Tim McCarthy jumped in front of Reagan, taking a bullet to his chest.

Ronald Reagan's letter to Tim McCarthy

RONALD REAGAN

September 17, 1993

Dear Tim:

There are hardly words that can adequately convey the friendship Nancy and I have for you. What began more than a decade ago as a routine government assignment has resulted today in one of the most important friendships Nancy and I have.

I will never forget that day in March of 1981 when our two lives became forever entwined. At that sudden moment outside the Washington Hilton, as the sound of shots rang out, you demonstrated the ultimate act of courage and bravery. I will always remember the sight of you throwing yourself in front of a mad man's bullet that was coming in my direction. I will be forever in your debt for that selfless act.

A time of crisis does not make or break a man, it only reveals him. And, what was revealed of you on that March morning shows the type of character you possess which has enabled you to succeed in 21 years of distinguished service to the United States Secret Service.

In addition to your acts of bravery on my behalf, Nancy is also deeply grateful to you for the fine job you did in protecting her those years in the White House.

We have heard of the wonderful job you will be taking in the private sector. We wish you and Carol every possible happiness in this new life.

We hope you will have more time to travel now and can make a trip out to California as we would enjoy the chance to see you again.

Sincerely,
Ronald Reagan

Special Agent Timothy J. McCarthy
United States Secret Service
Chicago, Illinois

Reagan and McCarthy both recovered in the hospital. McCarthy took little praise for his courage, crediting his Secret Service training. He said, "In the Secret Service, we're trained to cover and evacuate the president...it probably had little to do with bravery and an awful lot to do with the reaction based upon the training."

Ronald Reagan

Tim McCarthy

This photograph shows President Reagan moments before the shooting. After the shooting, two other agents pushed President Reagan into a car. Others captured Hinckley.

Close Call

Plenty of attempts on famous figures' lives have been successfully prevented by the Secret Service without bloodshed. The Secret Service doesn't like to reveal too much about these cases so enemies don't know how they operate. In 1996, President Bill Clinton was in the Philippines and ready to visit an official when his protective detail learned of mysterious messages being passed on radio channels. Two words stood out to them: "wedding" and "bridge." "Wedding" is sometimes a code word for an attack, and there was a bridge on the president's planned route.

The agents sent the president on a new route and then examined the bridge he would have taken. They found bombs! They had prevented an assassination.

The Secret Service now has special vehicles that can "jam" electronic signals that may be responsible for making bombs explode.

Could the Secret Service Have Saved JFK?

There were 28 Secret Service agents with President John F. Kennedy on November 22, 1963, in Dallas, Texas. That day, Kennedy was riding in an open car when he was shot twice by a man in an upper window of a nearby tall building. Some wonder if the Secret Service could have prevented this. Others blame Kennedy's wish to ride in the open car to greet people. Undoubtedly, this assassination forever changed the way Secret Service agents guard presidents.

The Secret Service Wants YOU!

Do you think you have what it takes to be a Secret Service agent? Your first step is to stay in school. Agents use knowledge of subjects you may be taking right now in their investigations: science, government, computer science, math, writing, and foreign languages. Agents need either a four-year college degree or a combination of school and criminal investigative experience. They also have to be physically fit and have no record of criminal behavior.

People accepted into Secret Service training spend 11 weeks at the Federal Law Enforcement Training Center in Georgia for the Basic Criminal Investigator Training Program. There, they and other future federal agents are taught about the law, train with weapons, and learn how to defend themselves. They must pass this training on the first attempt.

Secret Service agents on protective detail don't just watch the president. Sometimes they have to jog or bike with them!

After the first training school, future agents do another 16 weeks of Special Agent Basic Training in Washington, D.C. During this time, they learn skills to tackle their duties in the Secret Service two-part mission, including identifying counterfeit money and protection. Again, candidates must pass the training on the first try or they can't become agents.

Even after completing both training schools, agents continue to receive even more advanced training throughout their career. For example, those in the Canine Explosives Detection Unit train with their dog for another 20 weeks.

Agents who wish to work in protection have to complete two years of investigative work first. Many choose to stay in investigations rather than take on the long hours and travel duties of protection work.

The Secret Service uses dogs from Belgium called Belgian Malinois. The dogs train an extra eight hours every week and become a part of their handler's family.

High-Pressure Career

Secret Service agents keep watch over the White House around the clock. They fade into the background at major speeches and conventions, ready to jump into action if necessary. It's up to them to protect the government officials who lead our country. Other agents protect people at major events, such as the Super Bowl, without anyone noticing.

The pressure is always on Secret Service agents to perform their tasks perfectly. If they don't, it could be a matter of life or death. They work long days and travel great distances. Could you handle such a high-pressure, important job? With intense schooling and training, you could become a Secret Service agent—a great protector of our country and its people.

Glossary

assassinate: To kill someone for political reasons.

consciousness: The normal state of being awake and able to understand what is happening around you.

forensic: Relating to the use of scientific knowledge or methods in solving crimes.

investigation: The act of trying to find out facts about something, such as a crime.

magnetometer: A tool used to find the presence of metal.

microphone: An electronic device that can send sound to another device.

polygraph: An electronic device that measures physical events such as heart rate and is often used as a lie detector.

smuggle: To carry goods into a country secretly because they're illegal or to avoid paying a tax on them.

terrorist: One who uses violence and fear to challenge an authority.

Index

Websites